Contents

KU-213-144

Some words are printed in bold, **like this**. You can find out what they mean on page 30. You can also look in the box at the bottom of the page where they first appear.

Everyone is talking

Think. Type. Send. Today that is all it takes to send someone a message. It is fast and easy to **communicate**. But it was not always that way.

People have always wanted to communicate with each other. In the past, people used many different ways to communicate. People drew pictures. They made sounds. They wrote letters. Now people use computers to communicate with each other. They also use phones.

Computers have ▶ changed the way people communicate.

Ben,

Hey! We got back home today. The plane ride was long. Thanks for letting us stay with you.

Big news! Mum got the new job. It is so cool that I can tell you the news so fast. Mum says we are lucky. We do not have to wait for letters. A long time ago, people had to wait to hear the news. It took weeks just to get one letter. I am glad we have computers now.

I have to go now. Write soon!

Kate.

Ancient communication

In **ancient** (old) times, communication was simple. People used their hands to **communicate** with each other. They may have used sounds or simple words.

Some people drew pictures on cave walls. One of these caves is in Lascaux, France. The cave walls are covered with paintings. The paintings are more than 16,500 years old. They show animals like bison and deer. Some animals look like they are running and jumping. Scientists are surprised by how good these paintings are. Sometimes the artists also traced their hands on the wall. They drew lines and **symbols** that meant different things.

Discovery!

Four teenage boys discovered the cave at Lascaux in 1940.

3,000,000– 2,000,000 B.C.

First humans appear in Africa.

3,000,000 B.C.	2,750,000 B.C.	2,500,000 B.C.	2,250,000 B.C

ancient very old
symbol picture or letter that stands for something else

What do the paintings mean? No one is really sure. The paintings could be one person's view of the world. Maybe the artist wanted the hunting to be good. So the artist painted many animals.

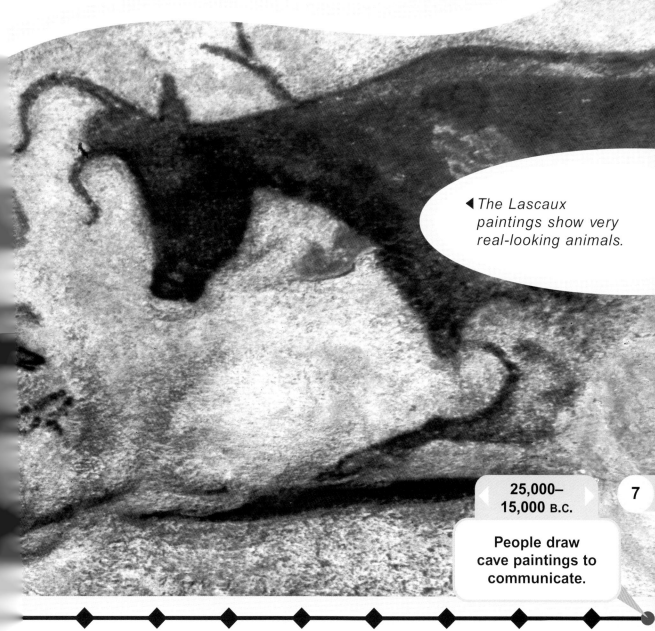

◀ *The Lascaux paintings show very real-looking animals.*

25,000–
15,000 B.C.

7

People draw
cave paintings to
communicate.

2,000,000 B.C. 1,750,000 B.C. 1,500,000 B.C. 1,250,000 B.C. 1,000,000 B.C. 750,000 B.C. 500,000 B.C. 250,000 B.C.

Using symbols

The Sumerians lived around 5,000 years ago. They **communicated** by drawing **symbols**. These symbols are called **cuneiform**. Cuneiform was the first written language. The Sumerians wrote cuneiform with a tool. The tool was called a **stylus**. A stylus is thin and sharp. They used it to write on wet clay. When the clay dried, the writing stayed on it for a long time.

Wet clay was good for ▼ writing. The writing could be erased.

3400 B.C.

The earliest Egyptian hieroglyphs appear.

3500 B.C.–
3000 B.C.

The Sumerian people invent cuneiform writing.

cuneiform	ancient Sumerian writing
hieroglyphic	Egyptian picture writing
stylus	sharp, pointed tool

3500 B.C.   3000 B.C.

The **ancient** Egyptians also lived around 5,000 years ago. The Egyptians used different pictures and symbols to communicate. Their writing is called **hieroglyphics**. It uses symbols called hieroglyphs (see picture below).

▼ *Egyptian tombs are filled with hieroglyphic writing such as this.*

1500 B.C.

The Phoenicians invent the first alphabet.

775 B.C.

The Greeks make their own alphabet.

2500 B.C.   **2000 B.C.**   **1500 B.C.**   **1000 B.C.**

Roman riders

By A.D. 100, Rome was the most powerful culture in the world. That was around two thousand years ago.

The Roman **Empire**, or government, ruled many lands. The Romans needed to **communicate** across the empire. They created the Roman postal service. Each Roman postal worker drove a cart. The cart was pulled by horses. The carts were filled with letters and packages. The workers carried the post across the Roman Empire. Some drivers travelled to nearby towns. Others travelled to cities hundreds of kilometres apart.

Roman roads

The Romans built more than 80,476 kilometres (50,000 miles) of stone roads. They were all built by hand.

600 B.C.

Books are made in China.

There were special stations along the road. Tired postal workers could stop at these stations. They got some food. They could sleep. Then they travelled on the next day.

▼ *The Roman postal service was called* cursus publicus *in Latin.*

105 B.C.	14 B.C.	11
Paper is invented in China.	The Roman postal service begins.	

B.C.   300 B.C.   200 B.C.   100 B.C.   0   A.D. 100

Communication in the Middle Ages

The **Middle Ages** was a time in history. It was from about A.D. 500 to A.D. 1500. That was from 1500 years to 500 years ago. In the Middle Ages, books were an important way to **communicate**. Some books were **religious**, such as the Bible. Others were about medicine and health. There were very few books around. Books were expensive.

Monks (religious men) wanted to save the knowledge in the books. So they made copies of each book by hand. They also drew beautiful pictures on the pages.

These copied books were sent to other places. Kings and wealthy people read the books. Teachers used the books. The information in the books was communicated to many people. People read books aloud to those who could not read.

No paper

In the Middle Ages, the pages of most books were not made of paper. They were made of animal skin.

500–1500

The Middle Ages.

Middle Ages	time in history from A.D. 500 to A.D. 1500
monk	man who believed in a higher power
religious	having belief in a higher power

500

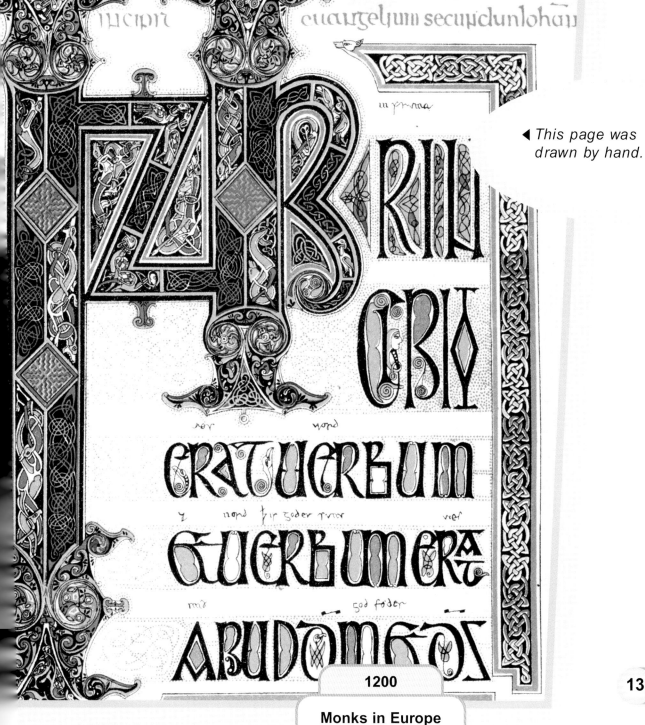

This page was drawn by hand.

1200

Monks in Europe make handmade books.

700   900   1100   1300   1500

A new invention

In about 1450, Johannes Gutenberg of Germany had an idea. It would change the world of communication forever.

At the time people still copied books by hand. Gutenberg thought this took too much time. He made letters and numbers out of metal. The letters could be lined up to form different words. People could put ink on the letters. Then they could press them onto a piece of paper to form words. This invention was called **moveable type**. Gutenberg built a special **printing press** for his moveable type.

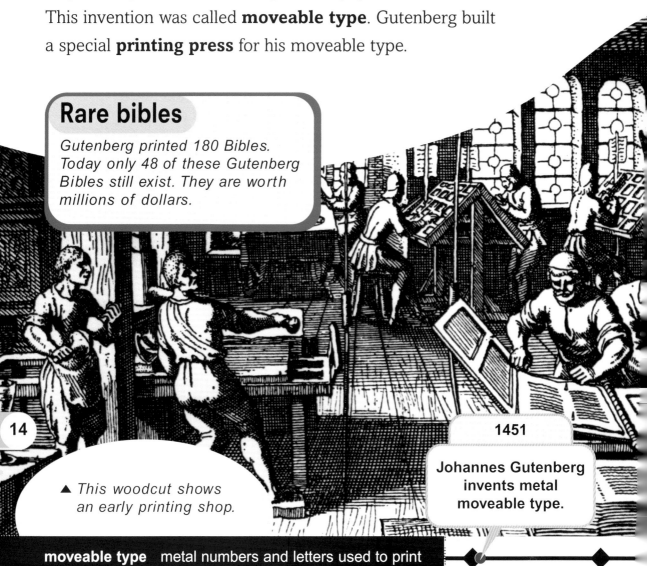

Rare bibles

Gutenberg printed 180 Bibles. Today only 48 of these Gutenberg Bibles still exist. They are worth millions of dollars.

▲ *This woodcut shows an early printing shop.*

1451

Johannes Gutenberg invents metal moveable type.

moveable type   metal numbers and letters used to print
printing press   printing machine

1450   1475

Soon Gutenberg's idea spread. For the first time, books could be made quickly. They cost less money to make. Thousands of books were published. More people could buy them. It was now much easier to **communicate** ideas through books.

▼ *Monks* in the *Middle Ages* used bright colours to paint book pages.

1500

More than 35,000 books are in print.

1565

The pencil is invented in England.

1500   1525   1550   1575   1600

Communicating in the New World

By the 1700s, thousands of people had settled in the United States of America (U.S.). Many big cities had their own printing shops. These shops printed one-page newspapers. The newspapers were called **broadsides**. Broadsides printed local news of the city.

At the time, the British ruled over America. America was made up of separate **colonies**. A colony is an area that is ruled by people from another area. Some people wanted to fight Great Britain for **independence**, or freedom. The broadsides spread these ideas. In 1775, the colonies turned against Great Britain. The Revolutionary War began.

1639

A printing press arrives in America.

broadside	one-page newspaper
colony	area that is ruled by people from another area
independence	freedom

During the war people counted on broadsides to get the news. Printers sent broadsides and books to many cities. Thousands of people read about the war.

Ben the printer

Benjamin Franklin lived in the United States of America. He was a printer, librarian, inventor, and politician (someone who helps to run the country). He learned to use a **printing press** at twelve years old.

▼ Broadsides helped people communicate information and ideas in the colonies.

1689

American newspapers called broadsides appear.

1775

The U.S. Postal Service begins.

1655   1680   1705   1730   1755   1780

Native American communication

Many Native American nations used smoke signals to **communicate**. Smoke signals told if there was good hunting in the area. They warned of danger. They were also a way to signal for help.

Smoke signals could ▶ be seen a long way over the Great Plains.

Native Americans first built a fire. They used damp grass or leaves. This made a lot of smoke. They put a blanket over the fire and then quickly took it off. This made the smoke rise in different shapes.

Special wood or plants also made the smoke change colours. The shapes and colours of the smoke communicated different messages. Other Native Americans could see the smoke signals from far away.

Native Americans also ▲ painted pictures on buffalo hides. Each picture told the story of an important event.

Communication goes West

Many Americans settled in west America in the 1800s. They wanted news from friends and family in east America. Letters were carried by people. It took months for one letter to travel from east to west.

The Pony **Express** opened in 1860. It carried letters, newspapers, and other written materials. The Pony Express went from St. Joseph, Missouri in the east, to Sacramento, California in the west. That is just under 3,000 kilometres (1,864 miles).

Special Pony Express stations were set up along the trail. Each Pony Express rider galloped from station to station. At each station the rider quickly jumped on to a fresh horse. A Pony Express rider could get news to the West in ten to fifteen days.

Fast track

In 1869, a transcontinental railroad was built. It was built across the United States of America. It linked the East Coast with the West Coast. The transcontinental railroad made communication very fast.

express   fast

▼ A Pony Express rider made about £50 a month. That's about £1,000 today!

21

Communication explosion!

In the 1800s, a lot of people invented new ways to **communicate**. The new ideas made communication faster. They made it easier and cheaper.

Typewriter

In 1867, the typewriter was invented. People could write words on paper, without a pen or pencil.

Morse code

In 1838, Samuel Morse created Morse code for telegraph. Each letter in the alphabet has its own set of dots and dashes.

1837

Telegraph is invented.

1838

Samuel Morse invents Morse code.

phonograph machine that records and plays sound

1830   1835   1840

Telephone

In 1876, Alexander Graham Bell invented the telephone. His experiment is famous. He shouted, "Mr. Watson, come here, I want to see you!" into a telephone. His friend Watson heard it from far away.

Phonograph

In 1877, Thomas Edison wrapped tin foil on a tube. Then he put a special needle against the tin foil. He turned the tube. He said the poem "Mary Had a Little Lamb." To his surprise, the **phonograph** had recorded his voice!

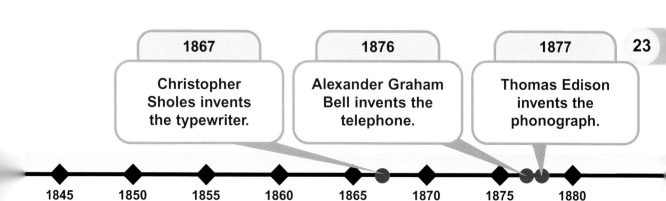

1867

Christopher Sholes invents the typewriter.

1876

Alexander Graham Bell invents the telephone.

1877

Thomas Edison invents the phonograph.

1845 1850 1855 1860 1865 1870 1875 1880

More inventions...

Moving pictures

In 1891, Thomas Edison built a machine. The machine recorded moving pictures. One of his first moving pictures shows a man sneezing.

Radio

Guglielmo Marconi sent the first radio signal. He was from Italy. The year was 1895. Another inventor, Nikola Tesla, also invented radio that year.

Tabloid newspapers

Joseph Pulitzer lived in the United States of America. He owned a newspaper called the *New York World*. It was different to other newspapers. It was called a **tabloid**. It had lots of photographs, cartoons, and advertisements. It was entertaining. By 1905, over two million copies were printed.

1891

Edison builds first moving pictures camera.

1895

Radio is invented.

1890   1900

tabloid entertaining newspaper that has lots of photographs, cartoons, and advertisements

Television

Philo Farnsworth had the idea for television. He was from the United States. He drew the plans for a simple television. In 1927, he built the first television set.

The Internet

The United States government invented the Internet in 1969. They wanted to use it to **communicate** in case of an emergency. The first users were scientists. By the 1990s, millions of computers were part of the Internet network.

1927

Philo Farnsworth builds the first television.

1969

ARPANET, the first Internet, goes online.

1910   1920   1930   1940   1950   1960

Communication in the Modern World

Today, people **communicate** in more ways than ever before. The biggest change in communication today is the computer. The computer has made communication easy and fast. **Billions** of people across the world use e-mail. They send messages with the touch of a button.

Ten years ago, very few people had mobile phones. Today it seems like everyone has a mobile! Mobile phones are not just for talking. People use mobiles for many reasons. They send and receive pictures. Some mobile phones can log onto the Internet.

These new inventions have changed how we communicate. It is now fast and easy to communicate with people anywhere in the world.

1973	1975
First mobile phone call is made.	First personal computers are sold.

billion number that equals one thousand million

1970   1975

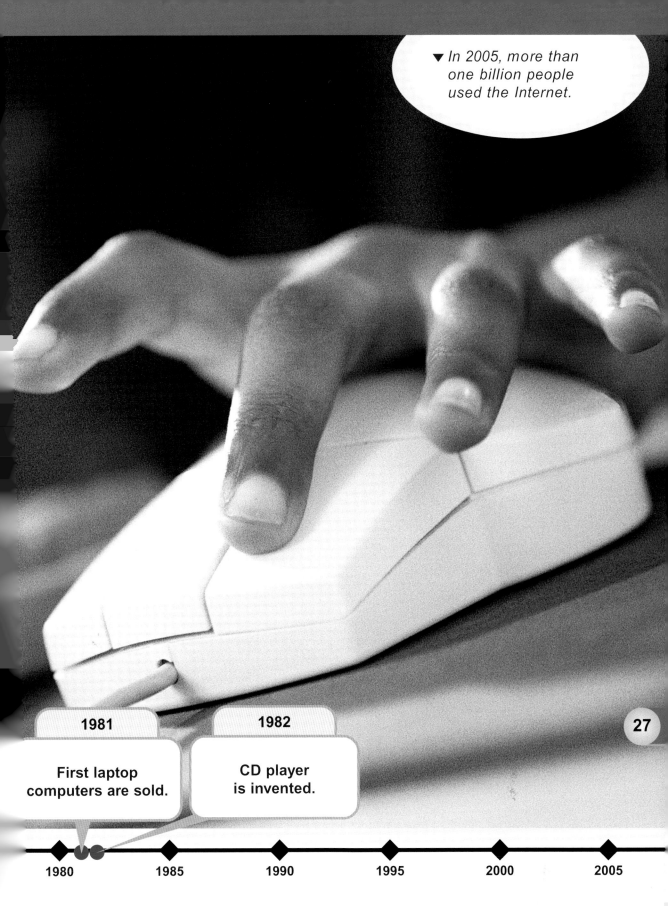

▼ *In 2005, more than one billion people used the Internet.*

1981

First laptop
computers are sold.

1982

CD player
is invented.

1980   1985   1990   1995   2000   2005

The future of communication

How will people **communicate** in the future? No one knows. Newer, faster, and easier ways of communicating will come along. Some will fade away. New inventions will change the world of communication again.

But people will always need to talk to each other. It does not matter if they use a computer. It does not matter if they use a pencil and paper. People will find a way to get their messages across.

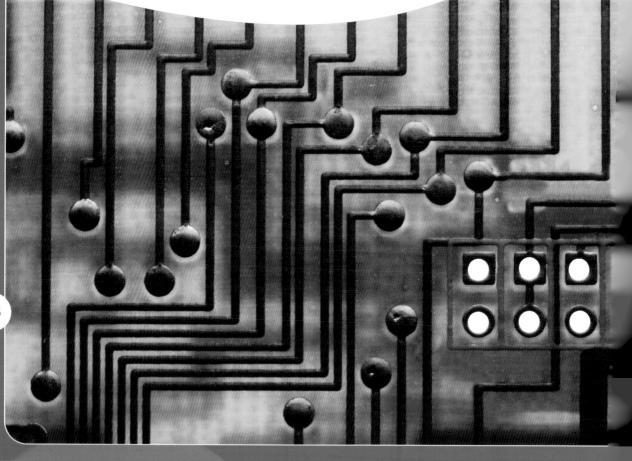

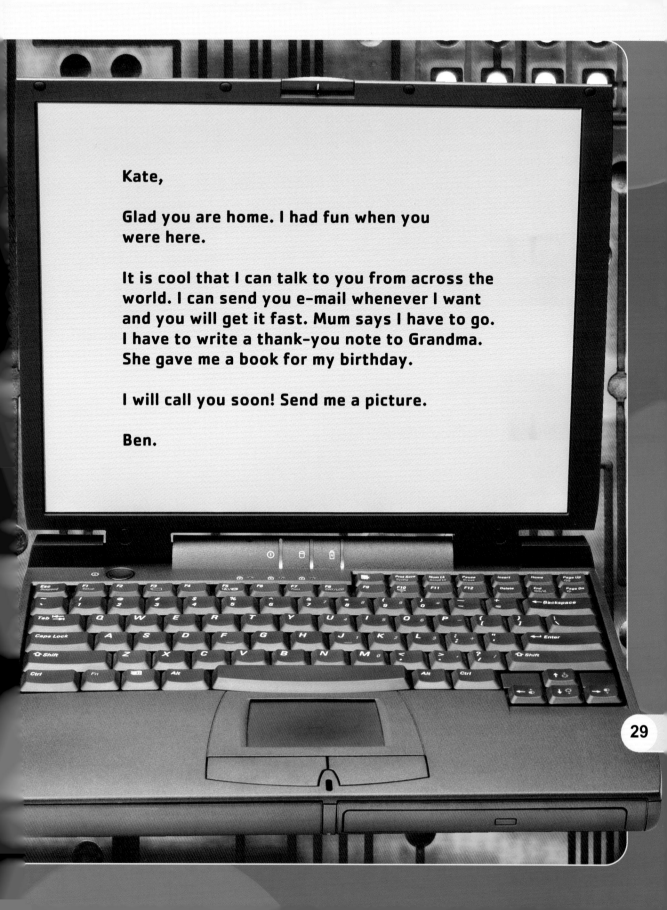

Kate,

Glad you are home. I had fun when you
were here.

It is cool that I can talk to you from across the
world. I can send you e-mail whenever I want
and you will get it fast. Mum says I have to go.
I have to write a thank-you note to Grandma.
She gave me a book for my birthday.

I will call you soon! Send me a picture.

Ben.

Glossary

ancient very old. The Ancient Egyptians lived a very long time ago.

billion number that equals one thousand million. There are more than 6 billion people in the world.

broadside one-page newspaper. During the Revolutionary War, Americans got information from broadsides.

colony area that is ruled by people from another area. In the early 1700s, Great Britain ruled over the American colonies.

communicate swap thoughts and ideas with another person. Computers are a fast way to communicate.

cuneiform ancient Sumerian writing. Scientists have found many very old clay tablets with cuneiform.

empire area that is controlled by a person or government. The emperor was the ruler of the Roman Empire.

express fast. Send a letter express so that it will arrive tomorrow.

hieroglyphic Egyptian picture writing. Ancient Egyptians wrote in hieroglyphics using symbols called hieroglyphs.

independence freedom. Americans fought for independence from the British in the Revolutionary War.

Middle Ages time in history from A.D. 500 to A.D. 1500. Knights fought battles in the Middle Ages.

monk man who believed in a higher power. In the Middle Ages, monks copied books by hand.

moveable type metal numbers and letters used to print. Moveable type was invented over 500 years ago.

phonograph machine that records and plays sound. The children listened to old phonograph records they found in the attic.

printing press printing machine. Modern printing presses are still used today to print newspapers.

religious having belief in a higher power. The Bible is a religious book.

stylus sharp, pointed tool. The Sumerians used a stylus to write cuneiform.

symbol picture or letter that stands for something else. Many road signs are symbols.

tabloid entertaining newspaper that has lots of photographs, cartoons, and advertisements

Want to know more?

Books to read

- *Communication: From Hieroglyphs to Hyperlinks*, by Richard Platt (Kingfisher, 2004)
- *Telecommunications*, by Anne Rooney (Franklin Watts, 2005)

Websites

- http://library.thinkquest.org/CR0211582/index.htm
  Check out communication inventions.
- http://library.thinkquest.org/5847/
  Find out about famous inventors and inventions.

Find your way around Earth's landforms, cities, and roads in *Lost!* There is a catch. You will only have a few maps, a ruler, and a compass. You will have your brainpower, too!

Be a storm tracker and track a hurricane from start to finish in *Storm Tracker*.

Index